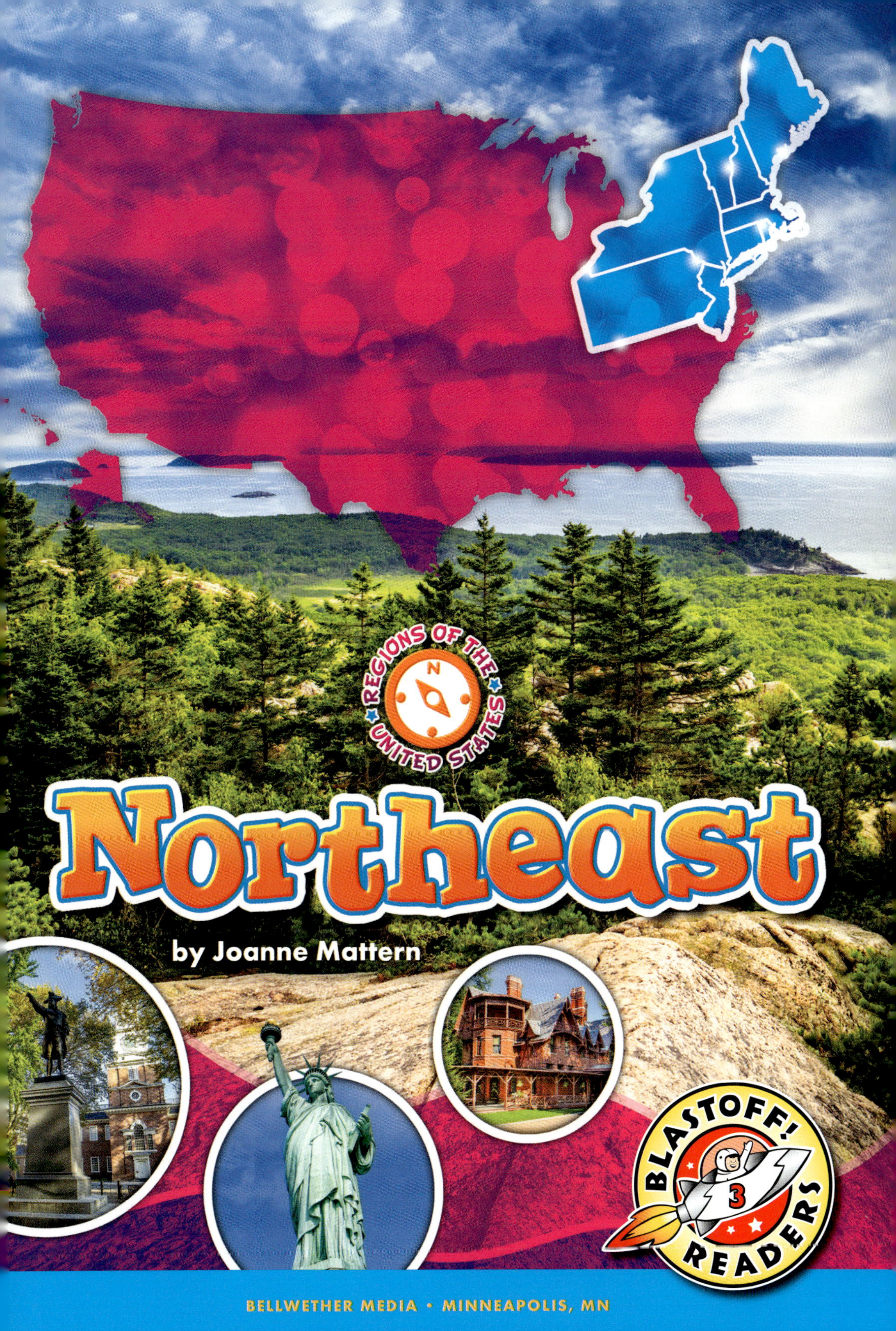

Northeast

by Joanne Mattern

BELLWETHER MEDIA • MINNEAPOLIS, MN

Blastoff! Readers are carefully developed by literacy experts to build reading stamina and move students toward fluency by combining standards-based content with developmentally appropriate text.

Level 1 provides the most support through repetition of high-frequency words, light text, predictable sentence patterns, and strong visual support.

Level 2 offers early readers a bit more challenge through varied sentences, increased text load, and text-supportive special features.

Level 3 advances early-fluent readers toward fluency through increased text load, less reliance on photos, advancing concepts, longer sentences, and more complex special features.

Reading Level

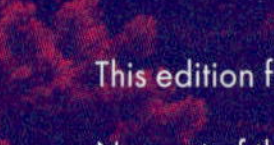

This edition first published in 2025 by Bellwether Media, Inc.

Library of Congress Cataloging-in-Publication Data

LC record for Northeast available at: https://lccn.loc.gov/2024039206

Editor: Kieran Downs   Designer: Brittany McIntosh

Printed in the United States of America, North Mankato, MN.

Table of Contents

Welcome to the Northeast!

The Northeast is a region of the United States. The region includes nine states.

Some of the 13 American **colonies** were in the Northeast. These colonies became the first states.

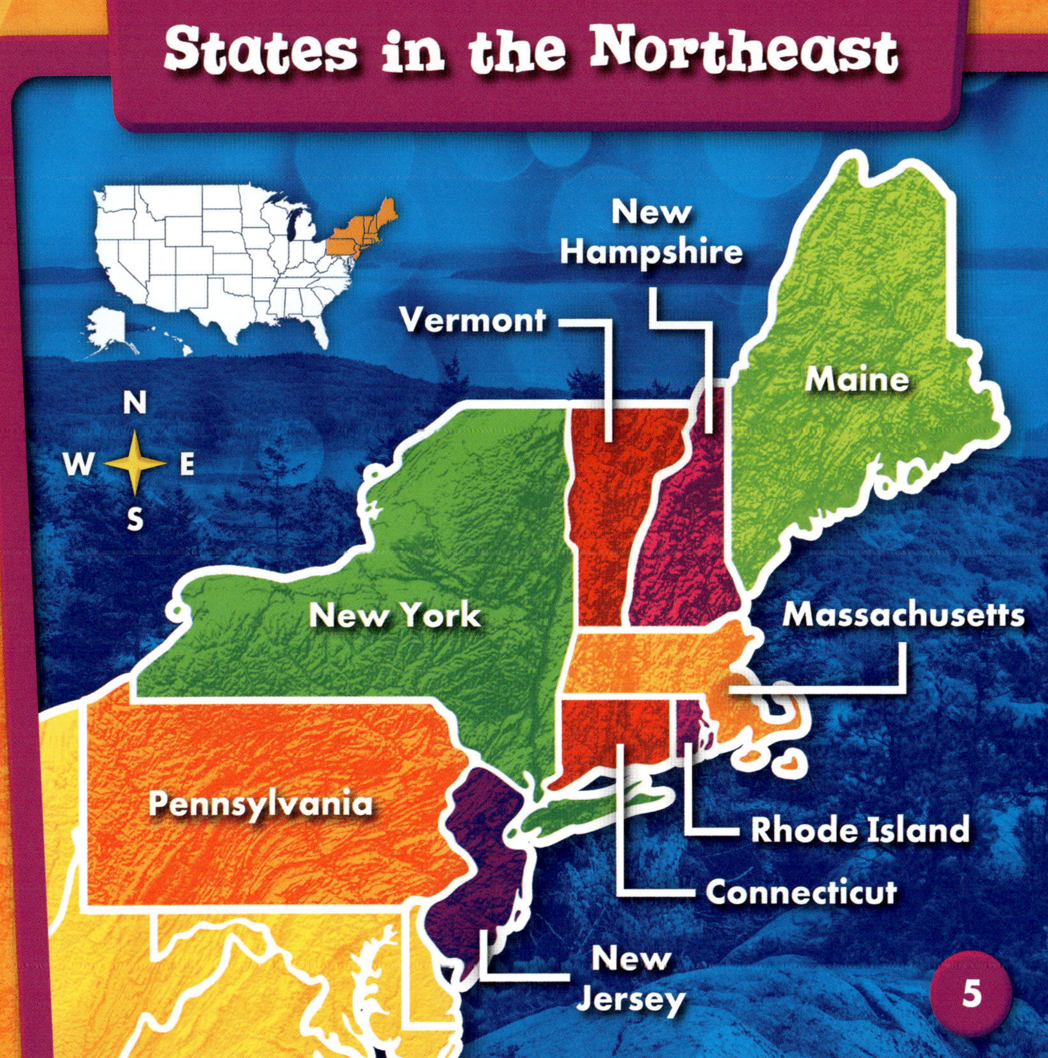

The Land, Weather, and Wildlife

Adirondack Mountains

The Appalachian Mountains stretch across much of the Northeast. The Adirondack Mountains stand in northern New York.

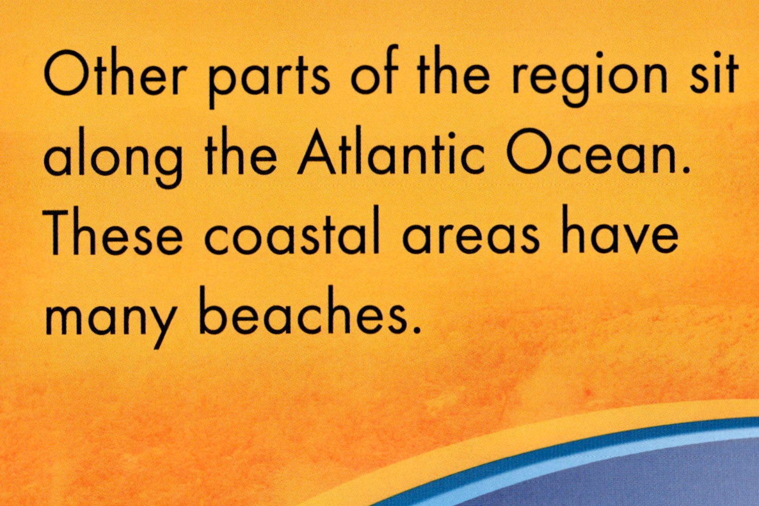

Other parts of the region sit along the Atlantic Ocean. These coastal areas have many beaches.

Atlantic
Ocean

The Northeast has a **continental** climate. Summers are hot and **humid**. Winters can be very cold.

Some places get a lot of snow. Areas around the **Great Lakes** often get more snow than other parts of the region.

Many animals live in the Northeast. White-tailed deer and black bears live in the forests. Fish swim in the rivers.

Many different birds call the Northeast home. Seagulls fly near the ocean. Piping plovers nest along beaches.

Natural Resources and Industry

Fishing is a large **industry** in the Northeast. Many people catch fish in the Atlantic Ocean.

Resource to Industry

Fishing

oceans

large fishing industry

dairy cattle

Agriculture is also important. People in the Northeast raise **dairy** cattle. They tap trees to make maple syrup. They grow many fruits and vegetables.

People of the Northeast

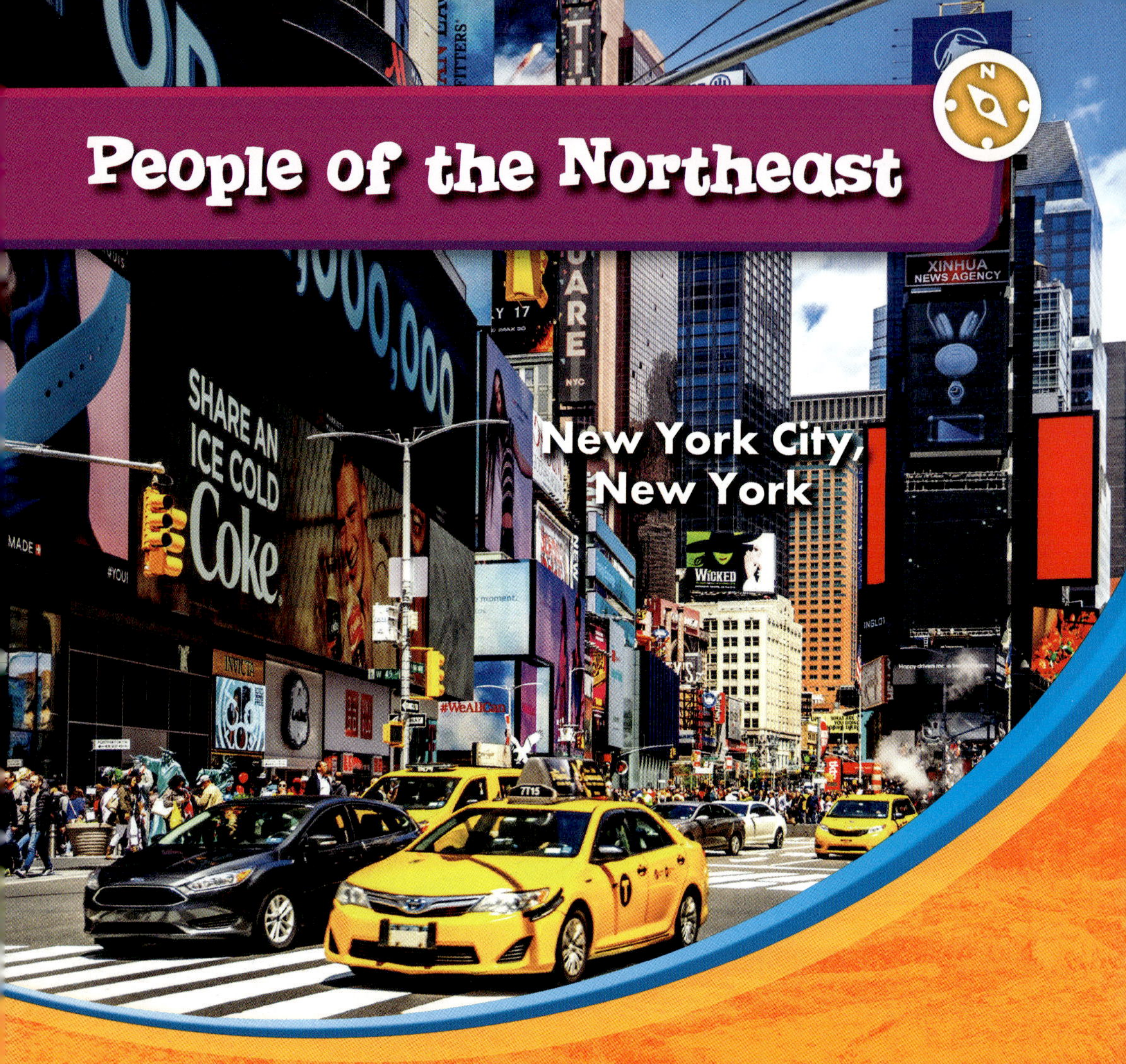

New York City, New York

Many Northeasterners have European **ancestors**. Others have Central and South American ancestors. Some have African ancestors.

Most people in the Northeast live in **urban** areas. The region is home to America's largest city, New York City, New York. Other people live in **rural** areas.

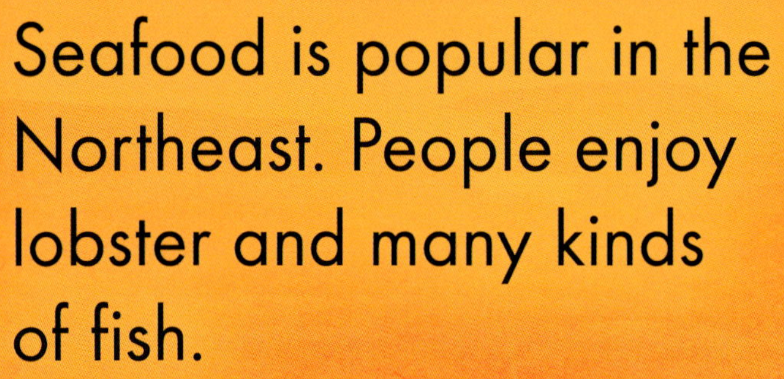

Seafood is popular in the Northeast. People enjoy lobster and many kinds of fish.

lobster roll

Sandwiches are popular, too. New York City is famous for deli-style sandwiches. Philadelphia, Pennsylvania, is known for its Philly cheesesteaks.

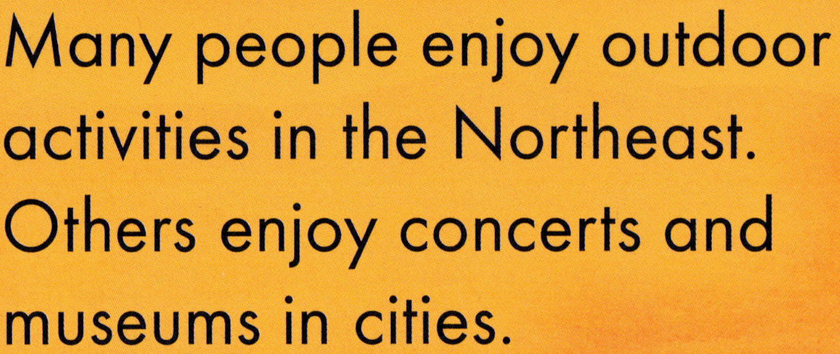

Many people enjoy outdoor activities in the Northeast. Others enjoy concerts and museums in cities.

People gather for holidays. New York City has a big Thanksgiving parade. Many cities have fireworks on the Fourth of July. There is always fun in the Northeast!

fireworks

Places to Visit
Independence Hall
Acadia National Park
Bar Harbor, Maine
N
W
E
S
New York City, New York
Philadelphia, Pennsylvania
Statue of Liberty

Northeast Fast Facts

3 Largest Cities (2020)

1 New York City, New York

Population: around 8.8 million

2 Philadelphia, Pennsylvania

Population: around 1.6 million

3 Boston, Massachusetts

Population: 675,674

State Populations (2020)

New York 20.2 million

Vermont 643,077

New Hampshire 1.4 million

Maine 1.4 million

Massachusetts 7 million

Rhode Island 1.1 million

Connecticut 3.6 million

Pennsylvania 13 million

New Jersey 9.3 million

Major Sports Teams

New York Yankees

(MLB)

Pittsburgh Steelers

(NFL)

Boston Celtics

(NBA)

Famous Face

Name: Taylor Swift
Hometown: West Reading, Pennsylvania
Famous for: Top-selling musical artist

Smallest State

Rhode Island
1,545 square miles
(4,002 square kilometers)

Largest State

New York
54,555 square miles
(141,297 square kilometers)

Glossary

agriculture—the practice of raising crops and animals

ancestors—relatives who lived long ago

colonies—distant territories which are under the control of another nation

continental—related to a climate with hot summers and cold winters

dairy—related to making food that is made mostly from milk

Great Lakes—large freshwater lakes on the border between Canada and the United States; the Great Lakes are Superior, Michigan, Ontario, Erie, and Huron.

humid—having a lot of water in the air

industry—a group of businesses that provide a certain product

rural—related to the countryside

urban—related to cities or city life

To Learn More

AT THE LIBRARY

Jacobson, Bray. *Niagara Falls*. New York, N.Y.: Gareth Stevens Publishing, 2023.

Leaf, Christina. *New York City*. Minneapolis, Minn.: Bellwether Media, 2024.

Spanier, Kristine. *Explore New England*. Minneapolis, Minn.: Jump!, 2023.

ON THE WEB

FACTSURFER

Factsurfer.com gives you a safe, fun way to find more information.

1. Go to www.factsurfer.com.
2. Enter "Northeast" into the search box and click 🔍.
3. Select your book cover to see a list of related content.

Index

The images in this book are reproduced through the courtesy of: Cheri Alguire, front cover (main); f11photo, front cover (bottom left, bottom right), pp. 19 (Independence Hall), 20 (Boston); lunamarina, front cover (bottom middle); Zeeking, p. 3; Marianna Campolongo, p. 4; Andy Williams photos, p. 6; Right Perspective Images, p. 7; DenisTangneyJr, p. 8; Sergii Figurnyi, p. 9; Tony Campbell, p. 10; Paul Reeves Photography, p. 11 (top); Pam Walker, p. 11 (bottom); Hitachy, p. 12 (left); Kyle Lee, p. 12 (right); Ron and Patty Thomas/ Getty Images, p. 13; Sina Ettmer Photography, p. 14; Steve Heap, p. 15; RFondren Photography, p. 16; Brent Hofacker, p. 17 (top); gkrphoto, p. 17 (bottom); Tetyana Ohare, p. 18; Universal Images Group North America LLC/ Alamy, pp. 18-19; Zack Frank, p. 19 (Acadia National Park, Statue of Liberty); phototrip2403, p. 20 (New York City); photosounds, p. 20 (Philadelphia); New York Yankees/ Wikipedia, p. 21 (Yankees logo); Pittsburgh Steelers/ Wikipedia, p. 21 (Steelers logo); Boston Celtics/ Wikipedia, p. 21 (Celtics logo); Brian Friedman, p. 21 (Taylor Swift); Mulevich, p. 23.